Uplifting Quotes for Trusting in God During Hard Times

By

Angelica Lassiter

Also by Angelica Lassiter

Confidence in God

ISBN-13: 978-1985723085

ISBN-10: 1985723085

<u>Acknowledgements</u>

This book is dedicated to those who believed in me and encouraged me to step out on faith. I would like to give a very special thanks to my late Great-Grandmother Willena (Mama) Andrews who allowed me to become connected with God at an early age by bringing me to regular church service and my sister Alysia for always being there for me when I needed her with my children.

Last and most definitely not least I thank my Creator above for blessing me to reach where I am today and where I am going only through His mercy, grace, and favor.

"Thank you, Lord for choosing and using me as a vessel to transform your message of love and hope to this world. You indeed deserve all the glory and honor forever!"

I love You, O Lord, my strength.
Psalm 18:1

Contents

Crying Out to God During Hard Times:

Psalm 40:1-4

1) *I waited patiently for the Lord; He turned to me and heard my cry.*

2) *He lifted me out of the slimy pit, out of the mud and mire; He set my feet on a rock and gave me a firm place to stand.*

3) *He put a new song in my mouth, a hymn of praise to our God. Many will see and fear the Lord and put their trust in Him.*

4) *Blessed is the one who trusts in the Lord, who does not look to the proud, to those who turn aside to false gods.*

Summary:

Though things may seem dark and stormy now, God is right there by your side waiting to umbrella and usher you through the rain, as He makes a way for gleaming sunshine to become your joyful gain; I encourage you to keep pressing forward and trust in His love.

We all face times where we end up in situations where we feel we have reached a dark cloud and are in pouring rain, drowning in our circumstances, feeling as though we will not be able to float and rise to the safe land of victory.

In this book, you will find comfort and solutions that you need to come out of dark situations as you submit to God and allow His power to pull you through, it all.

Introduction:

This book was created through the leading of the Holy Spirit to encourage and help you when facing hard times. To uplift and bring empowerment to break chains. To bring encouragement to your most inner thoughts, touch your most inner being, and through your faith, bring light, hope, power, and confidence to your deepest needs in a way that only the power of God can.

It contains a series of inspirational quotes given to me by God. My quotes are accompanied by a relational BIBLE verse, a summary of my quotes, and a reference prayer. I believe through activating your faith, this book will help bring the results you need and remind you regardless of the battles you face, you can trust in God to assist you to win every one of them.

After you read this book, I believe you will feel enlightened and encouraged to trust in God to be your source of comfort and love every day.

<u>Scriptures for Trusting in God During Hard Times:</u>

Trust in Him at all times; ye people, pour out your heart before Him: God is a refuge for us.
Psalm 62:8

Trust in the Lord with all your heart and lean not on your own understanding: In all your ways acknowledge Him and He shall direct your paths.
Proverbs 3:5, 6

<u>Quotes for Trusting in God During Hard Times:</u>

"When you trust in the Lord with your heart, He can mend and restore you as He intended to from the start"-
Angelica Lassiter

"Allow God to be the reason that you are able to speak your ability to rise above all odds has been discovered in this season. Trust in His love today"-
Angelica Lassiter

Chapter 1

<u>Trusting in Our God Who Comforts Us</u>

Scripture reference:

The Lord Himself goes before you and will be with you; He will never leave you nor forsake you. Do not be afraid, do not be discouraged.
Deuteronomy 31:8

Uplifting Quote:

"There may be times when you feel like you are on your last fuel and energy, feeling like you can't go on. During these trying times, I encourage you to turn to God; He's able to turn things around in your favor, so allow Him to become your comfort source today."

Summary:

Many times, we allow everything else but God to occupy our mind during hard times. Today, God wants you to release your burdens into His hands so that He can bring forth peace in your life as He has always planned; remain uplifted in His love.

Reference Power Prayer

Dear Heavenly Father,

I ask that You give me an extra boost of energy. I feel totally drained and I need You to strengthen me through Your love, might, and power. I thank you in advance for hearing my prayer in Jesus name, amen.

Scripture reference:

The righteous cry out and the Lord hears them; He delivers them from all troubles.
Psalm 34:17

Uplifting Quote:

"Always remember that God is waiting to take all your troubles, but you have to wholeheartedly release them to Him through prayer."

Summary:

Many times, we walk around feeling defeated and full of frustration due to life's troubles, storms, and trials. God wants you to know that He is waiting for you to release mental, financial, emotional, and physical burdens into His hands so that He can in turn, grant you joy and peace like only He can. So, I encourage you to release every burden to Him today.

Reference Power Prayer

Dear Heavenly Father,

I turn to You; crying out for You. I need help with my trials and my burdens. I ask that You remove this heaviness out of my life. I need deliverance and I need solutions, so I am asking You to grant me solutions to these draining matters. I declare my burdens have now been released to You. Please bring deliverance of the troubles that I face daily. Cause them to flee and take flight then grant me solutions as only You can in Jesus name, amen.

Scripture reference:

The Lord gives strength to His people; the Lord blesses His people with peace.
Psalm 29:11

Uplifting Quote:

"Feeling tired and worn out? Seek God's word and Him through prayer and allow Him to give you newly found rest, hope, and peace, even during your storms."

Summary:

We all face times when we feel conquered by our battles and it causes distractions. I would like to encourage you that you don't need to look anywhere else but to the comfort source of God who can bring forth great peace in your life as you allow Him to.

Reference Power Prayer

Dear Heavenly Father,

I ask that You give me strength and power to overcome the battles that I am facing. Father, I know You already have my situation worked out, I just need You to steer my mind away from my circumstances and into Your peace. Draw me to Your love. I trust You, love You, and believe that You have already given me victory, in Jesus name, amen.

Scripture reference:

"I will refresh the weary and satisfy the faint."
Jeremiah 31:25

Uplifting Quote:

"There may be times where you feel emotionally wiped out and drained, please always remember that God is waiting to release all of your anxiety, burdens and pain, so that all of your pain can be drained, then God can fill you up with all the joy, peace, favor, and healing that your heart can sustain as you submit to Him and receive it."

Summary:

Many times, we let circumstances in our lives get the best of us and it results in us being anxious, wiped out, and totally exhausted. I want to remind you that God can take your exhaustion and replace it with His incomparable peace if you would stop holding on to it; turn to Him and release!

Reference Power Prayer

Dear Heavenly Father,

I am constantly finding myself overwhelmed and exhausted with my life and the situations that I am facing. Father, I ask that You release my exhaustion; grant me solutions and add in my life peace which only can be provided through Your love. Thank you for granting me the refreshment that I need in Jesus name, amen.

Scripture reference:

Turn to me and be gracious to me, for I am lonely and afflicted.

Psalm 25:16

Uplifting Quote:

"There may be moments when you feel all alone, my advice to you during these trying times is to turn to God for comfort; trust in His uplifting power. He is able to bring forth the peace you need as He is preparing your best life possible."

Summary:

I am sure we all have been witnesses to seasons of loneliness. The great thing about God is that He is able to offer you the relief you need if you would just trust in Him enough to release your emptiness to Him and receive His plans for your life.

Reference Power Prayer

Dear Heavenly Father,

Please help me overcome loneliness. Father, although I know that You are with me at all times, I require a little extra attention in this area of my life. I ask that You not only grant me power to overcome this, but please create and surround me with an opportunity to be complete and Whole in every area of my life. Thank you in advance Heavenly Father in Jesus name, amen.

Scripture reference:

A time to search and a time to give up, a time to keep and a time to throw away.
Ecclesiastes 3:6

Uplifting Quotes:

"That moment when you decide to let go and let God can be the moment when His uplifting power can step in and amaze you by far."

"When you hold on to things that God has advised you to let go, it causes unnecessary pain and blocks God's best to show, so I encourage you to release and receive God's best today."

Summary:

Many of us battle with releasing things that no longer serve a purpose in our path; we act as our own blockage. Today, God is saying that He loves you so much; He is waiting to take every ounce of your baggage, heaviness, and loads, then bless you with something great as you trust in His power to do so.

Reference Power Prayer

Dear Heavenly Father,

Please remove everything in my life that is acting as a blockage to where You desire to lead me. Father, I thank you in advance for the doors headed my way upon me releasing every obstacle standing in my way, so I release my battles to You right now and receive by faith what is mine in Jesus name, amen.

Scripture reference:

Cast all your anxiety on Him because He cares for you.
1 Peter 5:7

Uplifting Quote:

"As you face various circumstances, instead of being anxious and worried, I encourage you instead to pray to God; believe that your circumstances are already resolved. I have discovered that worrying about things, followed by praying to God with belief of His graciousness, power, and love resulted in my worriedness being gone, with followed solutions. I encourage you to do the same and trust in Him today."

Summary:

Many times, our mind becomes attentive on worry rather than on God. Always remember that He can't fail. I encourage you today to release your problems to your problem solver. His everlasting favor can seal peace in your life like no other.

Reference Power Prayer

Dear Heavenly Father,

I ask You to renew my mind. Please remove worry and fear. Grant me joy, peace, and grace; bringing forth the solutions that I need. As I am seeking You and believing in my heart that You are leading me to great new doors of opportunity, I thank you in advance for Your favor soon manifesting in my life in Jesus name, amen.

Scripture reference:

"Come to me, all you who are weary and burdened, and I will give you rest: Take my yoke upon you and learn from Me, for I am gentle and humble in heart, and you will find rest for your souls."
Matthew 11:28, 29

Uplifting Quotes:

"Just when you may feel spiritually and mentally drained, God is able to step in and provide you with renewed strength that only through His power can be claimed. So, no matter what you face, always remember that God loves you; one touch of His favor is all that it takes to have powerful victory in your life, walk, and race if you just believe."

"Unexplained pressure may head your way but always remember that we serve an awesome God who is able to release grand loads off your life and uphold you in His presence in every form and way as you submit to Him and believe."

Summary:

There is no better way to become renewed and refreshed than to allow God to be your strength. Through His hands, your weariness can be uplifted, recharged, and rejuvenated as it is victoriously given through His love.

Reference Power Prayer

Dear Heavenly Father,

I ask that You provide me with the strength and refreshment I need to go on. I feel weary and I need Your rest so that I can continue to press forward and be my best. I humbly ask for Your help so I can be my best possible daily in Jesus name, amen.

Scripture reference:

He gives strength to the weary and increases the power of the weak.
Isaiah 40:29

Uplifting Quote:

"Weary, weighed down moments can become happy uplifted moments when you allow God to do the rising up and transitioning."

Summary:

Most likely we have all been weighed downed by life's circumstances which have grabbed ahold of our mind. Today, I encourage you to connect with and trust in God. He can make weary times joy filled times as you release every burden into His hands.

Reference Power Prayer

Dear Heavenly Father,

I ask that You release weariness out of my life. Please place in my life Your rest and Your peace. Weariness is taking a toll on me and it is weighing me down. I want to feel happy, fulfilled, and Whole again. I thank you for making me a conqueror through Your love and power in Jesus name, amen.

Scripture reference:

You have broken through all his walls and reduced his strongholds to ruins.
Psalm 89:40

Uplifting Quote:

"Always remember when it appears your situation has your back up against a wall, God is able to step in and perform a miracle which can cause every wall to fall in your favor if you just believe. Have confidence in His love today!"

Summary:

I am sure we have all faced situations where we were completely out of options and was unable to come up with a solution to resolve it. God wants to remind you today that if you would release your backed-up situation to Him, He is able to grant you a solution that only He can as you activate your faith to receive it.

Reference Power Prayer

Dear Heavenly Father,

Please tear down every wall that is standing in the way of me receiving Your best. Please block, remove, and tear down everything trying to block my access to the joy, peace, rest, favor, and territory You have prepared just for me. I come against defeat and claim victory over every area of my life in Jesus name, amen.

Scripture reference:

You have broken through all his walls and reduced his strongholds to ruins.
Psalm 89:40

Uplifting Quote:

"If you ever feel stuck, cornered, or bound over any past or present battle or circumstance, I want to encourage you that God loves you too much to keep you cornered and pinned against a wall over your past or present fiery trials; seek Him to release every stronghold today."

Summary:

God is able to cause even the strongest trials in your life to become solutional. There is no match that compares to His power. He confirms this through His powerful word. Never feel like your battles are a reason to doubt that God shall grant you victory. Trust in Him. Nothing will ever compare to His love and the plans that He has for you.

Reference Power Prayer

Dear Heavenly Father,

I turn Your way regarding these fiery trials that I am facing. I ask that You enter my situation with powerful force and tear down every wall attempting to hold me captive, blocking access to retrieval of Your promises. I declare according to Your word, my prayer, and my faith that I have been granted an immediate solution to my situation. I release this trial out my life right now in Jesus name, amen.

"Always remember our Heavenly Father loves you so much and is forever keeping you covered in His protective shield and blood. Trust Him because He's in total."
Angelica Lassiter

Chapter 2

Trusting in God Our Battle Shield

Scripture reference:

Finally, be strong in the Lord and in His mighty power:
Put on the full armor of God, so that you can take your
stand against the devil's schemes.
Ephesians 6:10, 11

Uplifting Quote:

*"Once you make the decision to be in the army of the Lord,
expect trials, and storms, but also expect your inner strength
to be an extraordinary tool, as well as your spiritual weapons
which are prayer, God's word, and His instructions in the
BIBLE, as well as praising Him to get you through. God has
already power equipped you with more than enough ability to
overcome every test and trial which heads your way so remain
strong, encouraged, determined, and blessed."*

Summary:

Once you enter in God's army, there is a war that goes
on that will try to wear you out and weigh you down,
making you feel overwhelmed and attempt to set you
on the wrong track. Please take this as a reminder that
God has already power packed and equipped your
steps, making you as His child able to fight back and
conquer every battle that heads your way. So
confidently trust in Him today.

Reference Power Prayer

Dear Heavenly Father,

While facing this war, I ask that You extend Your hand of help my way. Knock out every weapon that arrows and targets itself against me, attempting to knock me off the course. Also, as I prepare to fight back with all my spiritual tools of armor, I ask that You cast all my warfare away in Jesus name, amen.

Scripture reference:

For the LORD, your God is the one who goes with you to fight for you against your enemies to give you victory. **Deuteronomy 20:4**

Uplifting Quote:

"If you are facing battles, please know that God wants you free; He is ready to take over every situation, so why hold on to your battles when He is readily waiting to remove them out of your life?"

Summary:

True freedom is found in the power of God. Allow His power to give you the joy that you need. Open your heart and mind to receive His power, love, and rest. Release every battle to your shielding sword and see a constant solution provided through Him as He fights and wins every battle for you.

Reference Power Prayer

Dear Heavenly Father,

I ask that You fight for me. Win my battles for me. I am tired of fighting these battles alone and then finding myself constantly underachieving and losing. I believe according to Your word that I have the victory. I can't win this myself. I need Your freedom to reign upon every area of my life. Please free my mind, life, and remove everything attempting to come against me. Thank you for granting me everlasting favor and victory in Jesus mighty name, amen.

Scripture reference:

Blessed is the one who perseveres under trial because having stood the test, that person will receive the crown of life that the Lord has promised to those who love Him.
James 1:12

Uplifting Quote:

"Never allow your trials to cause resistance to your triumphs. Rather, fight the good fight; trust in the Lord with all your heart and know that through His love everything will be alright."

Summary:

God does not want frustration to overcome us, rather, He desires us to be conquerors through His love, might, and power, so allow Him to push you up and pull you out of all battles as you cast your cares upon Him today.

Reference Power Prayer

Dear Heavenly Father,

I ask that You give me an extra heaping of Your strength to overcome this battle that is going on in my life. Father, I know that I already have victory according to Your written promises but there are times when I feel like giving up. But I don't want to give up, rather, I want to lean on You, and allow You to give me the peace that You have promised me. Please pull me out of this and allow me to paddle through these trial waves using Your powerful arms as my strength. I love You and claim victory in every battle through Jesus's precious blood in Jesus name, amen.

Scripture reference:

"You are my hiding place; You will protect me from trouble and surround me with songs of deliverance:
"I will instruct you and teach you in the way you should go; I will counsel you with My loving eye on you."
Psalm 32:7, 8

Uplifting Quote:

"I know that many of us are struggling with something in our lives but the best way to start recovery and resolution is to give it to God."

Summary:

God is able to take your struggles, emptiness, missing pieces, and life imbalances and grant you in its place balance, resolutions, restoration, and peace as you trust in Him and allow His hands to act as a source of instruction and direction in your path.

Reference Power Prayer

Dear Heavenly Father,

I ask for Your help with my struggles. Please instruct me in the way to go. Bring deliverance by working out every passage that is causing me not to have full access to correct balance and direction. Keep me surrounded with Your guidance and love. Grant me alignment in my life that allows everything I am required to do to be done decently and in order. Help me fulfill every duty without complication in Jesus name, amen.

Scripture reference:

The Lord is a warrior, the Lord is His name.
Exodus 15:13

Uplifting Quote:

"Every day in the spiritual life is a battle but if you allow God to be your guidance and leader you will overcome any situation faced in life."

Summary:

As you face war in this race, always remember that God is our warrior, our strong tower, and victory is yours; please keep in mind that you are an overcomer as you honor and trust in Him. He has granted you access to the victory that has been promised to you when Jesus died on the cross for us.

Reference Power Prayer

Dear Heavenly Father,

I ask that You lead me as I face battles. I trust in You. I thank you for being my warrior. I thank you for the comfort You give me. I thank you for being my blanket of protection. Lastly, I thank you for allowing every weapon forming against me to be acquitted, destroyed, and never succeeding to prosper. I love You now and always in Jesus name, amen.

Scripture reference:

Though I walk in the midst of trouble, You will revive me. You stretch forth out Your hand against the wrath of my enemies. Your right hand will save me.
Psalm 138:7

Uplifting Quote:

"Spiritual warfare can be a real battle, but if you allow yourself full connection to God and gather up your spiritual weapons, all battles will be pushed out of your life and released into God's mighty loving hands, so I encourage you to let go and release to God today!"

Summary:

Spiritual warfare will always be something we must encounter. The Holy Spirit led me to remind you about the weapons God created for you to conquer your warfare. Keep them close and in constant ready use and find that they shall unleash the power needed to deteriorate all spiritual wickedness which heads your way so confidently trust in God's power.

Reference Power Prayer

Dear Heavenly Father,

Draw me close to You every day and even closer when the enemy sends his devices and schemes to attempt to set me off track and defeat me. Grant me discernment to identify the enemy's plots and schemes. Also, show me how to deal with his attacks by effectively using the tools that You have given me to overcome warfare and battles so that I don't grow weary and faint in the process in Jesus powerful name, thank you Father, amen.

Scripture reference:

Through You we will push back our adversaries, through Your name we will trample down those who rise against us.

Psalm 44:5

Uplifting Quote:

"Just when you may feel that your battles and warfare may never end, God is able to step in and fight your battles, striking all opponents of warfare out and victoriously granting you a new beginning. Claim victory over every single battle, attack, warfare, and setback and in return receive peace, joy, victory and breakthrough in your life as only God can if you believe. Trust in His amazing love today!"

Summary:

As you allow God to help you conquer your warfare and battles, as you open your heart to receive His help, He is able to strike every arrow aimed your way and transform it into a pile of useless dust. Then as every battle is trampled, He can give you a breakthrough of joy which is incomparable to what you can achieve yourself if you trust in Him enough to receive it. Seek Him and claim your victory today.

Reference Power Prayer

Dear Heavenly Father,

As these battles come against me and my enemies come against me, I want to say thank you for stepping in and causing them to be dodged out of my way. Please allow me to be continuously showered with Your presence, love, and favor. Thank you for causing everything that intends to bring harm my way to flee and go astray. Today, I claim all forms of victory in my life through this prayer in Jesus name, amen.

Scripture reference:

The Lord is a warrior, the Lord is His name.
Exodus 15:13

Uplifting Quotes:

"Always remember no matter what you face, God is able to allow you to overcome every battle in your life, walk, and race if you just believe."

"Always remember once you are planted in God's corner the battles are no longer yours, they are His."

Summary:

Believe in His might, trust in His unlimited power. Believe through Him, victory is yours.

Reference Power Prayer

Dear Heavenly Father,

I thank you Lord that You are a name of power. I thank you Lord that You are a name of peace. Today, I ask You to unleash Your power and peace upon every area of my life that needs victory. Lastly, I thank You for planting me in Your winning circle today and always in Jesus name, amen.

Chapter 3

Patiently Trusting in God

Scripture reference:

And my God will meet all your needs according to the riches of His glory in Christ Jesus.
Philippians 4:19

Uplifting Quote:

"Reveal to God all your needs and trust that He hears you and shall provide in your life like only He can."

Summary:

I am sure we have all experienced times where we've felt we reached the end of our rope, like we were unable to make it through another day because every resource we once had was all used up. God wants you to know that though it seems you have reached your limits, a point of nothing remaining, He is still able to provide to you a new thing; giving you a resource only He can bring forth in your life and lead you in a direction that will allow you to reach an experience that you have never known as you trust in Him to do so.

Reference Power Prayer

Dear Heavenly Father,

Please provide every need of joy, peace, healing, favor, restoration, prosperity and new beginnings in my life as only You can in Jesus name, amen.

Scripture reference:

But if we hope for what we do not have yet, we wait for it patiently.
Romans 8:25

Uplifting Quote:

"Never allow frustration due to God's timing to get you down. Rather, keep trusting in God to fulfill His promises as you wait patiently for His power to step in and change things around."

Summary:

I just want to remind you that though a blessing, door, or opportunity may tarry, God's word says that it shall come to pass according to His divine will and purpose. I encourage you to keep dreaming, keep believing, and keep trusting God to bring forth those dreams and desires in your life which will have an amazing impact. Remember that He's in complete control.

Reference Power Prayer

Dear Heavenly Father,

Please remove frustration I have while waiting on You. Supply me with support only You can give me. Be my midst of comfort and love every day. Keep my mind set on what You are getting ready to do rather than what I am facing right now. Thank you for keeping me surrounded by Your love, mercy, and grace every day of my life in Jesus name, amen.

Scripture reference:

Set your mind on things above and not on earthly things.
Colossians 3:2

Uplifting Quote:

"Always remember that every distraction can be an attraction to failure in life and reaching your goals and ordained purpose."

Summary:

Many times, we get distracted by things of this world or even things of non-importance and it can cause us to miss our divine appointed call and other great opportunities. I want to encourage you not to look to the left nor to the right but remain focused straight ahead in the direction God is leading you to as you submit, obey, and trust in Him alone.

Reference Power Prayer

Dear Heavenly Father,

Please help me keep my mind and focus set on You and what is best for me rather than being distracted by things of non-importance. Lead me in the way that will prevent me from stumbling and falling short of the intended purpose You have planned for my life. Thank you for helping me daily and staying by my side in Jesus name, amen.

Scripture reference:

Being strengthened with all power according to His glorious might so that you may have great endurance and patience.
Colossians 1:11

Uplifting Quote:

"God wants you to be patient with Him while He works out every area of your life for your good and His glory. So think about it, why get weary while you are waiting for your blessings?"

"Always remember that every good thing we receive which has a great long-term impact on us comes over time, so I encourage you to trust in God and wait in confidence!!"

Summary:

It is very important to have patience in your walk. The BIBLE describes many stories where different people received their inheritance following a period of waiting. Also, I would like to encourage you while waiting a beautiful thing to consider is that principles in your life can be discovered, our inner strength can fully develop, and the discovery of our inner abilities can unfold. So please trust in God and wait patiently on His promises to manifest in your life.

Reference Power Prayer

Dear Heavenly Father,

As I patiently wait for Your answer to my prayers, I ask that You help me find ways to discover the inner power You have given me. Also, show me ways to be greatly used by You. I also ask You to help me prepare for the solutions that You have planned just for me. With the help of the Holy Spirit, please let me be convicted enough to deny doing things on my own because I don't want to fall short, rather, I've decided to trust in You and be led by Your divine direction in Jesus name, amen.

Scripture reference:

Let us not become weary in doing good, for at the proper time we will reap a harvest if we do not give up. **Galatians 6:9**

Uplifting Quote:

"Just because it may appear at times you're not going to make it through, doesn't mean God's not right in the midst of your situations, setting up an appointed time for you to receive your breakthrough. No matter how impossible it may appear to reach where you ideally dream, God is able to allow you to accomplish all your dreams if you believe. "

Summary:

It's usually during the darkest times in our lives when we discover our inner power and even though it feels like we are going to tumble and fall, we find that God is faithful and is not only working behind the scenes on our behalf, but also, we find that He is the only one we need to reach our ideal dreams and retrieve victory. Once again patiently trust in Him and receive the harvest that is on its way.

Reference Power Prayer

Dear Heavenly Father,

Please forgive me if I have ever doubted You. Please help me tame my thoughts and remove any doubt during impossible seeming seasons of my life. I think back at how You've helped me before, and I know that as the unchanging God You are that You shall help me again. Please revive me during my period of waiting. I love You dearly and declare I shall reap victory in Jesus name, amen.

Scripture reference:

My God is my rock, in whom I take refuge, my shield and the horn of my salvation. He is my stronghold, my refuge and my savior- from violent people you save me: "I called to the LORD, who is worthy of praise, and have been saved from my enemies."
2 Samuel 22:3, 4

Uplifting Quote:

"Just when the waves of life feel like they're overpowering you; moving you further away from that safety gate you've always known as shore, God is in the process of redirecting you to a place that you've never known before. Lean upon His unchanging hand, God knows all your needs, just allow Him to show you that He's able to allow you to reach success and not lack any good thing as only He can."

Summary:

So many times, it can appear you are drifting away with no safety net, but God is actually taking you out of treacherous waves, away from your enemies, and those who are rising against you, and is sailing you to His safe haven, so trust Him to sail you to victory today.

Reference Power Prayer

Dear Heavenly Father,

As I face times when it feels like You are drifting me away, please help me openly receive Your direction and protection. I thank you for being my gate of safety every step of the way. I choose to trust where You have me right now and I thank you for where You are leading me through Your amazing mercy and grace upon my life in Jesus name, amen.

Chapter 4

Trusting in Our God Of love

Scripture reference:

The LORD your God is in your midst, a mighty one who will save; He will rejoice over you with gladness; He will quiet you by His love; He will exult over you with loud singing.
Zephaniah 3:17

Uplifting Quote:

"Always remember when the love and support of God is on your side, He can ensure that you are receiving a full portion of supply. So go ahead, plug into His unlimited power so that a wave of peace can be transferred your way as you lean upon your strong tower."

Summary:

God's love for you is unbreakable and most certainly He is in continuous motion for you, working on, through, and for you. He provides ways to supply your every need and see you through it all so embrace His love today.

Reference Power Prayer

Dear Heavenly Father,

Every place where I have lack I ask that You provide a way. Father, please show up in my midst, keep me covered and constantly surrounded with Your love. Stand beside me and show me how to abide by Your ways so that I can be comforted and provided the source which will keep me in total fulfillment in every form and way in Jesus name, amen.

Scripture reference:

"I love those who love Me, and those who seek Me diligently find Me."
Proverbs 8:17

Uplifting Quote:

"When you motion your life in the right source, a joy is received in your life which can't be forced; rather, given only through the love and power of God so, diligently seek Him with your whole heart today."

Summary:

Just want to remind everyone to make sure that you are leaning your life efforts and steps in a direction that has both natural and eternal rewards and the best place to begin is in God's Direction. Seek Him and get directed to the path of victory today.

Reference Power Prayer

Dear Heavenly Father,

Please move my life in the direction that will have a natural and eternal impact for my good and Your glory. I need You to show me how to allow my efforts to be of everlasting value and realize the only way this is possible is through Your love and direction. I ask that You direct my path and lead my way. I desire my life to reflect the way You have foreseen it before I was formed in my mother's womb. I thank you, love You, and will praise Your Holy name forever in Jesus name, amen.

Scripture reference:

For the sake of His great name the LORD will not reject His people, because the LORD was pleased to make you His own.
1 Samuel 12:22

Uplifting Quote:

"When the support of God is on your side, a power is released over your life which cannot secede as you seek Him with your whole heart, obey Him, and believe."

Summary:

God has promised that He will never leave nor forsake us. This promise is an attached covenant which ensures that abandonment will never come forth as we seek His Holy will, obey Him, and believe. I encourage you to turn His way and become a one of a kind vessel today!

Reference Power Prayer

Dear Heavenly Father,

Please help me keep my mind and heart attentive to Your will, so that Your covering is with me at all times, seeing me through. I need Your support and love. I can't make it without You. I give thanks to You for being my confidence and shield. Praise and honor is Yours because You deserve all glory forever in Jesus name, amen.

Scripture reference:

The LORD delights in those who fear Him, who put their hope in His unfailing love.
Psalm 147:11

Uplifting Quote:

"God's ability to transform your life, heart, and mind is endless, so trust in His unfailing love today."

Summary:

He is just an amazing way maker. Trust Him to make a way for you. He is proud to call you His own and is happy to provide for you in unforeseen ways. Those who are confident enough to diligently seek His will for their life are secure, so I invite you to become a product of the Lord today.

Reference Power Prayer

Dear Heavenly Father,

Please help me stand firm in Your unfailing love. Keep me in reach of Your amazing joy. Regardless of what heads my way, I am making a choice that I want to live in the loving fear of You. I want to be on fire for You and those things only You can offer me. I want Your joy and protection. I desire to receive Your love and do things the way You see fit for my life. Please allow Your power to keep me ignited, uplifted, protected, and secure in Jesus name, amen.

Chapter 5

Trusting God to Transform the Past for Your Good

Scripture reference:

For the word of the Lord is right and true; He is faithful in all He does.
Psalm 33:8

Uplifting Quote:

"God proves Himself faithful time and time again, so never think that His faithfulness will not show up this time and step in. Have confidence in His love today."

Summary:

God is the same yesterday, today, and always so never think that His goodness, love, mercy, and grace towards you, and power upon your life will ever change. Always trust in Him because He indeed is faithful.

Reference Power Prayer

Dear Heavenly Father,

Teach me how to count on Your faithfulness rather than the ground circumstances of situations I face in life. I trust Your proven mercy, grace, and love. I ask You to express it in my life every day; thank you for lavishing Your love upon me in Jesus name, amen.

Scripture reference:

Brothers and sisters, I do not consider myself yet to have taken hold of it. But one thing I do: Forgetting what is behind and straining toward what is ahead.

Philippians 3:13

Uplifting Quote:

"Stop putting focus on what you've lost and remain confident in what you have left; then put God in the midst of it and allow Him to shift you to reach your best blessed. Trust in Him because He is able."

Summary:

God is so much greater than your shortcomings and the places you have fell short in life. He has a plan to remove the scars of your past and give you restoration as only He can, so trust in Him and believe.

Reference Power Prayer

Dear Heavenly Father,

I ask You to remove every spiritual and natural blindfold that is keeping me blinded with thoughts of what occurred in my past. Please remove them so I can clearly see the path You have prepared to take me into my bright future. I trust in You and Your word that clearly states that greater is coming then what has already came, so I thank you in advance that it is already done in Jesus mighty name, amen.

Scripture reference:

"Forget the former things; do not dwell on the past.
Isaiah 43:18

Uplifting Quote:

"Learn to leave the pain of yesterday in yesterday so that it doesn't interfere with the bright potential of today."

Summary:

There are so many things that God wants to add in your life, but first, He needs you to heal from your past. Start releasing your past to Him so that He can begin opening the doors that He has planned for today, and all your days. Stop being a victim of what already occurred, so God can send in your life what He has in store as you seek Him with your whole heart, obey, and trust in Him alone.

Reference Power Prayer

Dear Heavenly Father,

I ask that You remove the pain of my past. Release it in Your hands so that I can begin preparing for enjoyment of the great things You have planned for me. I declare going forward, I am no longer a victim but instead, I am a victorious winning servant with a bright future. In Jesus name, I receive my new and forget my former amen.

Scripture reference:

"So if the Son sets you free, you will be free indeed"
John 8:36

Uplifting Quote:

"Many people feel trapped and chained by yesterday's mistakes, please know that there is no mistake you can ever make that God's love and power can't restore or break. Seek Him today and see for yourself that He loves you unconditionally and will make a way by ordering your steps and setting you on the path to victory."

Summary:

There is absolutely no reason you should feel chained down when God loves you so much and sent His son to set you free. Stop allowing the past to be your reason to not reach the greatness of your future and walk into the freedom that Jesus has given you today.

Reference Power Prayer

Dear Heavenly Father,

I turn to You and ask that You break the chains that have kept me bound up until this point in my life. I declare I am living and walking as a new creation because I believe in the power Your word carries. As I was brought with a price, I speak the promises You already pre-assigned for me shall begin manifesting IMMEDIATELY in Jesus mighty name, amen.

Scripture reference:

I consider that our present sufferings are not worth comparing with the glory that will be revealed in us.
Romans 8:18

Uplifting Quote:

"Always remember that every past and present failure can never compare to the joy, peace, and love that God has for you and your heart desires He wants to come to pass as you seek Him with your whole heart, obey Him and believe. "

Summary:

God confirms through His word that every suffering you bear on this Earth is going to bring forth a divine reappointment of joy if you keep pressing forward, positioning yourself, and believing that through faith, focus, obedience, submission, and confidence, His reward is great for all who love Him.

Reference Power Prayer

Dear Heavenly Father,

Please help me bear the pain, sufferings, and burdens that I am facing. Through Your word, promises, and love, I ask You to keep me comforted. Your word confirms that the joy You have revealed surely will come to pass if I remain strong and obedient to Your Holy will. I thank you as I trust in You, I will be able to one day look forward to Your unspeakable joy and blessings being released in my life, in Jesus name, amen.

Scripture references:

Let your eyes look straight ahead; fix your gaze directly before you.
Proverbs 4:25

Do not conform to the pattern of this world but be transformed by the renewing of your mind. Then you will be able to test and approve what God's will is- His good, pleasing, and perfect will.
Romans 12:2

What good is it for someone to gain the whole world, yet forfeit their soul?
Mark 8:36

Uplifting Quote:

"Never cheat your future by trying to re-live and return to your past, rather trust in God because greater is coming."

Summary:

There is nothing that the world could have given you before Christ that God has not already prepared greater for you. I want to encourage you to let your past go, let those sinful desires go, let unnecessary pain and suffering go. Trust God to give you a new life pattern where His love can flow, and your best blessed path can show. Receive the plans that He has for you today.

Reference Power Prayer

Dear Heavenly Father,

I ask that You access my life and help me. Please remove my desires that oppose Your will. Today, I choose to let my past go and resist what no longer fits in my life and means me no good. Those things which have served their purpose in my path, please remove them now. I am making better choices and choosing to no longer compromise; please remove those desires from my heart. I ask that You lead me to my intended purpose in Jesus name, amen.

Scripture Reference:

Therefore, if anyone is in Christ, he is a new creature; the old things passed away; behold, new things have come.

2 Corinthians 5:17

Uplifting Quote:

"Always remember what God has removed out your life and swept away, is nothing compared to what He is preparing to send your way as you submit to Him, trust Him with your whole heart, and believe."

Summary:

God has already done a new thing in your life as you became a product of Him through Jesus Christ so embrace your new identification today.

Reference Power Prayer

Dear Heavenly Father,

I ask as You have given me new identity through Jesus Christ, that I embrace it wholeheartedly and begin walking in my new light. Please allow me to openly and without further delay receive the new walk that You have promised me. I thank you for removing every smear and blemish that my past has marked upon me. I thank you for cleansing me through Jesus's precious blood in Jesus name, amen.

Chapter 6

Having Complete Faith and Trust in God

Scripture reference:

'If you can?" said Jesus. "Everything is possible for one who believes."
Mark 9:23

Uplifting Quotes:

"Sometimes you got to have crazy faith because God can't fail!"

"Have faith, trust God, work hard, and despite all obstacles every detail of your dreams shall take flight."

Summary:

Faith is assurance of a win for those who trust in Him.

Reference Power Prayer

Dear Heavenly Father,

I come against everything attempting to waver my faith. I declare that my faith and trust in You is in full force and everything I am believing You for, those things I can only imagine You have planned for me, what I thought would never occur in my life are beginning to come to pass TODAY in Jesus name, amen.

Scripture reference:

"But I trust in Your unfailing love; my heart rejoices in Your salvation."
Psalm 13:5

Uplifting Quote:

"God's just as amazing at hard times as He is at joyful times. Never allow the condition of life circumstances to condition your love, thoughts, trust, and confidence in Him. Remember, regardless of your situation, His plans for you are predestined and unchanged, He is just waiting for you to trust Him with your whole heart and call on His Holy name. Regardless of what you face on Earth, remember your reward in Heaven is guaranteed as you stay on the path of righteousness and obey His Holy will."

Summary:

God delivered incomparable power when He sent Jesus to die for our sins. His love for you is everlasting and adaptable to overcome and overturn to victory so always remember, despite what occurs in your life that victory is yours.

Reference Power Prayer

Dear Heavenly Father,

Please keep me in remembrance of the love You showed towards me when You sent Jesus to die for my sins. I ask You to keep me protected as I work daily towards my soul salvation in Jesus name, amen.

Scripture reference:

What then, shall we say in response to these things? If God is for us, who can be against us?
Romans 8:31

'If you can?" said Jesus, "Everything is possible for one who believes."
Mark 9:23

Uplifting Quote:

"Truly having faith in God means believing EVEN THE IMPOSSIBLE will come to pass so believe and claim it right now in your life."

Summary:

There are times when what appears is the impossible, is actually God setting up the possible. Stand on His word and believe that behind the scenes, He is working everything out and performing great works in your life as only He can.

Reference Power Prayer

Dear Heavenly Father,

I declare no matter how impossible this situation seems, just the fact that You are a God of impossibility, I am standing in confidence and complete trust in You to grant me breakthrough as only You can, in Jesus powerful name, thank You for giving me favorable results hallelujah, amen.

Scripture reference:

"I am the LORD, the God of all mankind. Is anything too hard for me?"
Jeremiah 32:27

Uplifting Quote:

"Sometimes you got to have faith that sees brightness in blind appearing situations; trust God to streak sunshine through every storm and trial."

Summary:

We've all heard stories and perhaps may have even witnessed times where God used faith to open blind eyes, raise the dead, heal bodies, and more. I want to encourage you to trust Him to fulfill that same power in your life. I pray today as you are believing Him to do it, He performs mightily and unleashes a great portion of joy, peace, victory, and favor in your life in Jesus name.

Reference Power Prayer

Dear Heavenly Father,

I declare I am safely planted in Your hands. By faith, I take back everything the enemy stole from me. By faith, I speak You have already given me uncommon favor. Lastly by faith, I speak that the same power You have shown towards others shall also be shown in my life. I believe miracles, signs, and wonders have already been pre-approved and are being released in my life RIGHT NOW in Jesus name, amen.

Scripture reference:

"But as for you, be strong and do not give up, for your work will be rewarded."
2 Chronicles 15:7

Uplifting Quote:

"When you are ready to give in and give up is usually when your miracle is in position and ready to show up, for His glory. Never give in or give up! Rather, remain trusting in the power of God to grant you a new beginning as you believe."

Summary:

Another reminder; when we are completely at the end of our rope, in total frustration, this usually is a sure sign that we are at the verge of a breakthrough that's right around the corner. So please, allow His written promises to seal your trust in Him that your reward is coming.

Reference Power Prayer

Dear Heavenly Father,

I trust in You. I believe Your word, Your promises, and Your divine counsel. I am letting You know that I won't give in and I surely won't give up. I will Never stop believing You for my breakthrough, and right now, I'm going to praise you in advance and rejoice because I believe that I am about to receive it RIGHT NOW in Jesus powerful name, amen.

Scripture reference:

What then, shall we say in response to these things? If God is for us, who can be against us?
Romans 8:31

"If you can?" said Jesus. "Everything is possible for one who believes."
Mark 9:23

Uplifting Quote:

"If you want to come to pass in your life something new, step out on faith and trust that the power of God shall step in and see you through it all. Have confidence in His love today."

Summary:

God acts in our lives according to our faith. Many times, we may find that things are not changing for us because we are not believing Him enough to press hard and receive change. I encourage you today to reach for the stars. You deserve a grab at every level of favor that has been predestined yours as His child so climb towards new heights today.

Reference Power Prayer

Dear Heavenly Father,

I declare according to Your word and my faith that things are changing. The things You have planned for me are now within my reach. I am stepping out and asking You to show me how to receive them. Show me the way to go and lead me in the right direction. No longer will I stand around and miss what has already been promised mine. Instead, I am reaching for the stars as the star You created me to be. I trust that You will help me reach my greatest potential I possibly can reach. I thank you for ordering my steps and making my ways prosperous daily in Jesus name, amen.

Scripture references:

Let all that I am wait quietly before God, for my hope is in Him.
Psalm 62:5

The Lord will fight for you; you need only to be still."
Exodus 14:14

Uplifting Quotes:

"God is the only one who can transform your pain into a delightful gain if you have faith; trust in Him and believe."

"Never take God's silence as a sign that you are being ignored. Many times, it is a blessing in disguise that is in process of fully developing a breakthrough in your situation, just trust in Him and praise Him as if it's already done."

Summary:

Never think just because God seems silent that He is absent. Please remember just because we can't see the things He is doing, for example, we can't see the air outside functioning and flowing but it is working properly doing its job and giving us fresh air. During hard times, trust in Him and His word. Praise and honor Him; set an atmosphere of preparation for Him to give you divine breakthrough as only He can.

Reference Power Prayer

Dear Heavenly Father,

When I face times where it seems You are nowhere to be found, when I feel like I'm doing this all alone, and it appears impossible for me to receive a breakthrough, I want to let You know that I have faith in You and I trust in You. I believe Your power is upon every area of my life. I believe the promises I read in Your word, and I declare that breakthrough will soon show up in my life and make it appear that my storms have never occurred in Jesus name, amen.

Chapter 7

Leaning on Our God Whom We Love and We Trust

Scripture reference:

But He said to me, "My grace is sufficient for you, for my power is made perfect in weakness." Therefore, I will boast all the more gladly about my weaknesses, so that Christ's power may rest on me: That is why for Christ's sake, I delight in weaknesses, in insults, in hardships, in persecutions, in difficulties. For when I am weak, then I am strong.
2 Corinthians 12:9, 10

Uplifting Quote:

"When experiencing trials and difficulties in your life, I encourage you to seek and build a relationship with God. While building your relationship with Him, you will discover not only will He guide you to your intended purpose, but also over time He will diminish your trials, while blessing your now and supplying all your needs during your process of transformation. So, seek Him to get started today."

Summary:

God is a God of transformation. No matter how good you think you can handle things on your own, you will never be able to match what He can do. He is waiting to transform your life inside and out. So let it go, release it, stop trying to handle things on your own. You've been through enough alone. I encourage you to seek God. Give your life to God. Build a relationship with God. He has plans for you that you've never known existed.

Reference Power Prayer

Dear Heavenly Father,

I turn to You during my time of trials. I release them to You. I desire to have Your solution granted to my situation. If I don't already have a personal relationship with You, I ask that it begins now. I thank you not only for transforming my situation, but first and foremost, I thank you for transforming my heart and mind and giving me victory through Your love in Jesus name, amen.

Scripture reference:

For the moment all discipline seems painful rather than pleasant, but later it yields the peaceful fruit of righteousness to those who have been trained by it.
Hebrews 12:11

Uplifting Quotes:

"Sometimes God allows us to hit rock bottom, so we can discover He is all we need to be Whole, so be encouraged and trust Him during every season of your life."

"Many times, God takes away what we think we need only to show us that His love is all that we will ever need. Trust Him to bring you out greater than you were before."

Summary:

It is usually during the toughest seasons in our lives when we are pruned and blossomed into a great tree of righteousness. I want to remind you that even if God has allowed you to reach a point where you feel you have lost everything you thought you ever wanted, God would never remove something out your life without a greater purpose, a greater appointed call or divine outcome that wouldn't bring you out greater than you were before. Embrace these hard times, get in your word and allow God to create you into the masterpiece He intended you to be.

Reference Power Prayer

Dear Heavenly Father,

Although I am facing a time where it feels I've reached one of the lowest points of my life, I want to let You know that I believe in You and that I trust in You. I believe according to Your word, I am on my way to receiving the biggest breakthrough that my life has ever experienced. I just ask that You point me to the direction where I can reestablish my steps so that I will never hit rock bottom again, in Jesus name, amen.

Scripture reference:

Be merciful to those who doubt.
Jude 1:22

Uplifting Quote:

"I encourage you to make a vow to never doubt God, know that His love for you is everlasting, His hand upon your life is never changing, and He is able to step in and bring out the best in you and see you through it all if you believe."

Summary:

This is a daily confession I encourage we all activate:

"I resist every thought, level, and action of doubt in Jesus powerful name, amen."

There will be times where it seems no matter how hard we pray, how much we try to do things according to God's will, how much we try to change something in our lives, or how much we sow for a breakthrough, it seems nothing works, and we find ourselves stuck in an unchangeable situation. I want to encourage you that God's love overrules every burden, situation, and chain. Never doubt God. Rather, trust Him to grant you power to fight the good fight through your faith. Speak life and remember, it has got to get better because He indeed is faithful.

Reference Power Prayer

Dear Heavenly Father,

I confess no matter how much it appears my situation will never change, I stand firm on Your word and promises. I declare by faith not only is my situation changing, but I believe You will grant me favor that is going to shift my entire life and change things for better. I am standing in confidence of Your word and claiming my new beginnings RIGHT NOW in Jesus name, amen.

Scripture reference:

So do not fear for I am with you; do not be dismayed, for I AM your God. I will strengthen you and help you; I will uphold you with My righteous right hand.
Isaiah 41:10

Uplifting Quote:

"Though we all face struggles, the great thing about following God is that all struggles are leading towards victory, never defeat, so I encourage you to continuously trust in our Heavenly Father every day."

Summary:

God allows struggles to come in our lives to help strengthen us and lead us to victory. He never intends or will allow them to harm or defeat us. Trust that He will never leave your side. Instead, He will uplift you in His strength, so allow yourself to be covered and crafted in His love today.

Reference Power Prayer

Dear Heavenly Father,

Please help me as I face struggles in this life. Allow me to lean on Your hand rather than being weighed down by my battles. Remove every stronghold attempting to hold me down, and instead, keep me covered and uplifted in Your strength, with Your power, and through Your love as You shift and direct me to victory in Jesus mighty name, amen.

Scripture reference:

"Ask and it will be given to you; seek and you will find; knock and the door will be opened to you.
Matthew 7:7

Uplifting Quote:

"God will never allow a problem to come in your life without a solution so seek Him with your whole heart and trust in His unlimited power because He loves you."

Summary:

God already prepared solutions to all your problems. The key to many solutions is to seek Him and ask Him to reveal the way to overcome them. Many times, the solution seems impossible because we haven't asked Him to show us the way to solve it. I encourage you today to ask Him to open doors that will unlock solutions to every matter.

Reference Power Prayer

Dear Heavenly Father,

I ask for solutions to the problems that I am facing. I am knocking on the door of Heaven through my prayer and ask that You rectify things rapidly and without any complications. I thank you that You are my solution maker and are always there for me when I need You in Jesus name, amen.

Scripture references:

Have I not commanded you? Be strong and courageous. Do not be afraid; do not be discouraged, for the Lord your God will be with you wherever you go."
Joshua 1:9

Be on your guard; stand firm in the faith; be courageous; be strong.
1 Corinthians 16:13

Uplifting Quote:

"Bravery comes when you come into full acknowledgement that through the power of God all battles are already won."

Summary:

One thing you must believe is that God is going to get you through your trials. He will keep His word. The vows He made to you will not be broken. No matter what you are facing always remember that God is in your race, directing you. However, we must stand strong and obey His will. Remain encouraged, determined, and blessed knowing that every weapon planned shall fail.

Reference Power Prayer

Dear Heavenly Father,

I ask for strength in my weaknesses despite what heads my way. Your word confirms that I should remain strong and courageous in You, so I declare that I have Your guard and strength at all times. Also, please give me the bravery I need to face and win what I must face as I go about each day, in Jesus name, amen.

Chapter 8

Trusting in God Who Is Our Stress Releaser and Peace Giver

Scripture reference:

Cast all your anxiety on Him because He cares for you.
1 Peter 5:7

Uplifting Quote:

"Your saddest moments can become your happiest moments when you allow God to do the transitioning of them."

Summary:

God provides the greatest joy. He has shared with us His greatest gift, our greatest comforter, the Holy Spirit who ushers us out of every level of grief. He has ushered me out of some very difficult situations and is waiting to also provide that same peace your way. Release your burdens to God through prayer, then if you desire, ask Him to give you the gift of the Holy Spirit and begin to receive your greatest level of comfort available in the Universe.

Reference Power Prayer

Dear Heavenly Father,

I turn to You and ask You to remove my sadness. I know I was not created to be sad, but to be happy. I can't break this wave of pain without You and I don't want to. Rather, I desire it to be broken by You so that I know that it will be completely gone. So, please remove all my sadness right now in the name of Jesus, amen.

Receiving the Holy Spirit

Scripture references:

But the Advocate, the Holy Spirit, whom the Father will send in My name, will teach you all things and will remind you of everything I have said to you.
John 14:26

And I will put My Spirit in you and move you to follow My decrees and be careful to keep My laws.
Ezekiel 36:27

All of them were filled with the Holy Spirit and began to speak in other tongues as the Spirit enabled them.
Acts 2:4

For all who desire the Holy Spirit, please speak the following prayer:

Reference Power Prayer

Dear Heavenly Father,

I desire to have the Holy Spirit in my life. I invite His presence in through this prayer and ask you to bring Him in my life so that the greatest comforter can be part of my life to comfort, direct, and guide me going forward in Jesus name, amen.

****IMPORTANT****

Upon asking God to release the Holy Spirit in your life, I recommend that you attend your next available church service and receive full portion access of the Holy Spirit at God's Holy altar. Please reveal to the head leader in your church (Pastor, Bishop etc..) that you desire to receive the Holy Spirit and have already prayed for God to place Him in your life. God bless.

Scripture reference:

You make known to me the path of life; You will fill me with joy in Your presence, with eternal pleasures at Your right hand.
Psalm 16:11

Uplifting Quote:

"When the presence of the Lord is in your life, it accompanies a wave of peace that brings forth an amazing delight, so I encourage you to bring forth His joyful presence through submitting in prayer today."

Summary:

There is absolutely no explanation to what God is able to provide your way through His peace and love. He's able to fill great joy inside of you. Trust in Him. Seek Him to receive His peace which is out of an explanation content today.

Reference Power Prayer

Dear Heavenly Father,

Please fill me up with Your peace which surpasses all understanding. Grant me the honor to be surrounded and engraved with Your joyful presence. I want to be filled with Your joy and love every day of my life. Please keep me guided by Your direction forever in Jesus name, amen.

Scripture reference:

Then they cried out to the Lord in their trouble, and He brought them out of their distress.
Psalm 107:28

Uplifting Quote:

"Never allow the storms in your life to bring frustration your way and tear you down, rather trust in the Lord and ask Him to step in and change things around just as He has promised you."

Summary:

Many of our storms can be described as little deposits where God is just rearranging some of our situations for better. The revelation God is advising me to tell you for help during hard times is to think about a blender when you are making a smoothie. Half way through the process of your ingredients, if you turn off the blender the food looks incomplete and unusable for the intention you placed it in there for. But once it's finished then it becomes one complete combination of a delightful beverage.

Well think about your own life this way, just because it may be whisking right now, once God steps in, everything will be leveled and right. Keep reminding yourself this and let yourself be daily whisked (in the spirit) and divinely ordered by God.

Reference Power Prayer

Dear Heavenly Father,

I ask for Your help during my time of distress. I am claiming Your promises through Your word that You will pull me out of this and grant me peace in my storm. I thank you for being my peace in every situation in Jesus name, amen.

Scripture references:

The Lord Almighty is with us; the God of Jacob is our fortress.
Psalm 46:11

Be strong and courageous. Do not be afraid or terrified because of them, for the Lord your God goes with you; He will never leave you nor forsake you.
Deuteronomy 31:6

Uplifting Quote:

"If you ever feel you are being forsaken or abandoned by God and He is not hearing your prayers, I want to encourage you that it is impossible for God not to make a shift in your life, to leave you in that same condition and circumstance, and not work things out for you if you have faith and trust Him with your whole heart and obey His Holy will."

Summary:

God promises us in His word that He has plans for us (Jeremiah 29:11). I want to encourage you He is preparing His plans for you and you are not alone; you are not losing your battle, God has not forgotten about you. He indeed is working behind the scenes and when He is finished your best outcome shall show. Keep trusting in Him, keep seeking Him, and above all keep believing that at the right time all you have faced shall make sense.

Reference Power Prayer

Dear Heavenly Father,

As I face this battle and feel shaken and worn, I ask that You lead me to Your plans, allow me to be given a glimpse of what is coming my way. I love You and do not desire to go astray from where You want me to be. Today I've decided to abandon the feeling that I am being forsaken and declare that You got me covered and my bright future is near in Jesus powerful name, amen.

Scripture references:

You Lord, keep my lamp burning; my God turns my darkness into light.
Psalm 18:28

Your word is a lamp for my feet, a light on my path.
Psalm 119:105

Uplifting Quote:

"Sometimes it appears that things will never change because your atmosphere appears all gloomy and black, please be assured that God truly loves you and is willingly waiting to assist you by bringing peace, joy, healing, and restoration back in your life as you allow Him to light your path; give Him your heart and believe."

Summary:

Even if it appears you have blackness in your life and can't see ahead, God has faithfully provided a light source for our every need through His word, submitting to Him in prayer, and obeying Him. Use all these tools to get the light source needed to succeed both naturally and eternally.

Reference Power Prayer

Dear Heavenly Father,

I ask that you direct my path. Remove darkness out my life. Shine Your marvelous light upon me. Remove every dark wave. I am willing to hear and obey what You have to say to me that will change my life for better. I ask that You lead me in the direction which will cause a great turn of favor to become my portion in Jesus name, amen.

Chapter 9

Trusting in God Who Makes A Way Out of No Way

Scripture reference:

Now to Him who is able to keep you from stumbling, and to make you stand in the presence of His glory blameless with great joy.
Jude 1:24

Uplifting Quote:

"Sometimes God allows your situation to reach a point where it seems hopeless so that it can be victorious in a way only He can provide. Never underestimate His power and have faith, trust, and confidence in Him today."

Summary:

God allows us to face encounters in our life beyond our control to remind us that He has and always will be able to bring victory in our paths. Never letting us stumble, but rather, allowing us to be overcomers through His love. Please take this as confirmation that no matter what appears hopeless, with God on your side, everything is already worked out.

Reference Power Prayer

Dear Heavenly Father,

As I am facing this situation, I declare according to Your promises that I have joy and I have peace. As I speak by faith, I now receive it. I also declare that no matter how impossible it appears for me to come out of this situation, I receive Your promises of deliverance and victory. I love You and thank you for pulling me through in Jesus name, amen.

Scripture reference:

No temptation has overtaken you except what is common to mankind. And God is faithful; He will not let you be tempted beyond what you can bear. But when you are tempted, He will also provide a way out so that you can endure it.
1 Corinthians 10:13

Uplifting Quote:

"When you seek God wholeheartedly there is absolutely no situation that He will not give you an escape from."

Summary:

We should remind ourselves this over and over again, God is a gentleman and has already prepared solutions to all our problems, however, we must first invite Him in to help us. I encourage you to stop trying to provide yourself an escape route. Submission to God is key not only to escape your now troubles, but to reach conclusions only God can provide for every trouble you ever face in life. Doing it God's way also prevents you from falling into tempting traps which can cause regret later. I encourage you to do it God's way first so that it will carry out correctly.

Reference Power Prayer

Dear Heavenly Father,

I invite You to take over my problems and ask You to grant me solutions that only You can. I choose not to do this alone because I desire it to be done correctly. Please also give me an escape route and strength to avoid falling into temptation which may cause me to slip rather than to overcome my situation in Jesus name, amen.

Chapter 10

Trusting in God Our Provider, God Our All

Scripture reference:

The lions may grow weak and hungry, but those who seek the Lord lack no good thing.
Psalm 34:10

Uplifting Quote:

"You may experience times where you feel you are in a season of lack, but always remember that we serve an awesome God who loves us, whom we can count on according to His word, promises, and power to step in even at the last minute and present an unexpected blessing which will result in your season receiving a major comeback. Trust Him because He never fails."

Summary:

God can supernaturally supply any need and bring forth joy where you can be freed. Trust Him because He is able to perform great works in your life.

Reference Power Prayer

Dear Heavenly Father,

As I am standing firm in faith throughout this journey, I ask You from the bottom of my heart to remove all lack from my life and give me a portion of oversupply as only You can in Jesus name, amen.

Scripture reference:

He stilled the storm to a whisper; the waves of the sea were hushed.
Psalm 107:29

Uplifting Quote:

"Just when the waves of life seem like they're going to wipe you out, God is able to step in WITH FORCE and bring forth a wave of peace that wipes the waves out in your favor as you believe; have confidence in His love today."

Summary:

God would never allow what is happening in your life to overpower you and knock you off course. He will allow you to overflow with peace instead. When facing burdens, speak by faith the stillness that the power of God can bring in your life and place a demand for it to be activated and watch our Heavenly Father grant you the peace that you need.

Reference Power Prayer

Dear Heavenly Father,

I declare I am taking authority over my storms. According to Your word, You hush the waves, even the greatest wave by Your voice and I speak by faith that every wave in my life is now overturned with Your peace. I speak through Your power planted inside of me that every peace blocker and raging wave is now removed out of my life in Jesus name, amen.

Scripture reference:

The lowly He sets on high, and those who mourn are lifted to safety.
Job 5:11

Uplifting Quote:

"Always remember to lift up the only one who is able to lift you out of every pit and into His glorious delightful presence."

Summary:

God wants to be acknowledged. He wants attention. He wants your praise. He reminds us in His word that He created us to be the apple of His eye, His masterpiece; He uses our praise to uplift and shift things in our lives; I encourage you to use your own God inherited gifts and talents to uplift Him and receive breakthrough today.

Reference Power Prayer

Dear Heavenly Father,

Teach me how to improve my relationship with You through uplifting and praising Your Holy name. Show me how to be more sensitive to Your requirements of me. I desire a stronger relationship with You and I am thankful that my own submission to Your will shall also bring me out of what I'm going through. I love You now and forever in Jesus name, amen.

Scripture reference:

The Lord is my strength and my defense; He has become my salvation.
Psalm 118:14

Uplifting Quote:

"Life has a way of sometimes trying to weaken or knock you down; but always remember that God is your strength, your mechanism of favor. He is waiting to step in and change things around in your favor, so have confidence in His love today."

Summary:

Life has points where it sets us on uneven tracks. But the great thing about God is that He is able to step in and provide you with every ability to set order and regain power back. Trust that He will allow you to retrieve your best outcome today.

Reference Power Prayer

Dear Heavenly Father,

I ask that You grant me balance in every unbalanced area of my life. Please take every uneven pattern and transform it into the sturdiness that I need; place my steps on sturdy ground and grant me divine order and direction. Lastly, please tear apart everything that is tearing away perfect peace in my life in Jesus name, amen.

Scripture reference:

Do everything without grumbling or arguing.
Philippians 2:14

Uplifting Quote:

"Life is too short to waste time bickering and letting yourself down. Instead of placing energy into useless complaining, I encourage you to uplift the mighty name of God who can step in and change things around in your favor! Remain encouraged in His power today."

Summary:

We are all on Earth for a reason and our days are numbered by God. Our time is limited and short. It is very imperative to stop using it unwisely with complaining. Begin preparing for what's to come and allow God to order your steps so that everything can be done effectively.

Reference Power Prayer

Dear Heavenly Father,

Please forgive me for times when I complain. I admit I come across times where I allow life to get the best of me, so I complain rather than seeking a solution from You. Today, I've decided to change my focus and allow my energy to be used for a greater source which is Your will, so I'm coming to You asking for Your assistance in helping me become victorious through making positive change in Jesus name, amen.

Scripture references:

For I am convinced that neither death nor life, neither angels nor demons, neither the present nor the future, nor any powers: Neither height nor depth, nor anything else in all creation, will be able to separate us from the love of God that is in Christ Jesus our Lord.
Romans 8:38, 39

You will keep in perfect peace those whose minds are steadfast, because they trust in You.
Isaiah 26:3

Uplifting Quote:

"God is greater than your circumstances so trust in Him today."

Summary:

Don't allow your circumstances to have you feeling out of position to fight back; trust that the power God provides is the only source needed to win every battle.

Reference Power Prayer

Dear Heavenly Father,

Sometimes life makes me feel hopeless and like I have reached out of boundary. I ask that You help me climb out of my circumstances and allow me to have peace and order in every area of my life in Jesus name, amen.

Scripture reference:

You are the God who performs miracles; You display Your power among the peoples.
Psalm 77:14

Uplifting Quote:

"Never think that God is not able to take over your situations and perform miracles in your life."

Summary:

I am sure that we have all faced times where we had some Very difficult situations occur and impossible seemed to be the only way to describe what we believed would be the result of it. The Holy Spirit is revealing today that if you would wholeheartedly trust God, He is able to transform possible out of every impossible according to your trust, faith, and obedience to His divine will. Activate more faith in your walk and allow more of His miracle working power to be seen in your life.

Reference Power Prayer

Dear Heavenly Father,

I speak by faith according to Your word, promises, and through my obedience and submission to You that every situation in my life that requires a supernatural miracle, sign, and wonder shall begin to manifest NOW in Jesus powerful name, amen.

Chapter 11

Praising God's Holy Name

Scripture references:

Let everything that has breath praise the LORD. Praise the LORD.
Psalm 150:6

Let them praise Your great and awesome name—
He is Holy.
Psalm 99:3

Yet You are enthroned as the Holy One; You are the one Israel praises.
Psalm 22:3

Uplifting Quote:

"There are miracles in your praise so place a supernatural shift in your life by pushing it through uplifting the powerful name of God today!!"

Summary:

When we speak, something happens, a zone comes forth, and that zone can be a powerful breakthrough source if you allow your voice to be an instrument of praise. God is ready to motion your breakthrough so activate your faith and let your voice speak victory in your life today.

Instead of prayer, let's all praise His Holy name!!!

Scripture reference:

The Lord is my rock, my fortress and my deliverer; my God is my rock, in whom I take refuge, my shield and the horn of my salvation, my stronghold.
Psalm 18:2

Uplifting Quote:

"Snap yourself out of a defeated mindset, having continued patterns of pain and release your frustration to God through prayer, He wants to give you a joyful gain. Quit trying to fight your battles alone when God is waiting to take over your burdens and grant you victory that can't be given anywhere else as you seek His Holy throne."

Summary:

God wants you to stop living life feeling defeated. Allow Him to provide a way by granting your solution. He specializes in providing for you so give Him access by seeking Him today.

Reference Power Prayer

Dear Heavenly Father,

Please remove my pain and feelings of defeat. I need this negativity erased off my mind. I am ready to move forward and receive the peace You desire me to have. Through this prayer, I declare I am receiving the solutions You have prepared just for me. Thank you in advance for the joy and peace soon to come in Jesus name, amen.

Chapter 12

Trusting in God Who Gives Us Victory Over Defeat

Scripture references:

"Do not seek revenge or bear a grudge against anyone among your people, but love your neighbor as yourself. I am the Lord."
Leviticus 19:18

Bear with each other and forgive one another if any of you has a grievance against someone. Forgive as the Lord forgave you.
Colossians 3:13

Uplifting Quote:

"Life is too short to allow pointless things to steal your happiness; let pointless grudges go and seek God to regain peace in your life."

Summary:

Stop allowing yourself to be linked to things which add no true value or work towards fulfilling God's purpose and plans for your life when He is trying to give you a new focus and grant you His solutions and peace.

Reference Power Prayer

Dear Heavenly Father,

Please forgive me for any grievances and grudges that I have toward others. Please detach them off my mind and from my heart. I want to let the past go and live in peace with all men as You require me to. Also, please forgive others for all the wrong that they have done to me. Following this prayer, I ask You to grant me a new beginning as only You can in Jesus name, amen.

Scripture references:

No, in all these things we are more than conquerors through Him who loved us.
Romans 8:37

"For My thoughts are not your thoughts, neither are your ways My ways," declares the Lord.
Isaiah 55:8

Uplifting Quote:

"A defeated mindset equals a defeated life so instead of allowing life obstacles to place you in fear and overpower you, why not choose to release everything to God who is able to provide you with divine restoration."

Summary:

Many of us fall short because we tend to give in and give up; settling for less than we deserve and what God desires for us to receive. God wants you to know that if you would snap out of that thinking pattern, think positive and tell Him you are willing to trust Him enough to give you what you deserve then He can bring the very best in your life.

Reference Power Prayer

Dear Heavenly Father,

Please help me tame my thoughts and train my mind to work on achieving my goals rather than focusing on the problems that try and overpower me. I desire to have the best in life which is Your best. Help me change my thought pattern so that I can receive the blessings that I deserve. I thank you for hearing my prayers and even greater thank you so much for answering them in Jesus name, amen.

Scripture reference:

What, then, shall we say in response to these things? If God is for us, who can be against us?
Romans 8:31

Uplifting Quote:

"Always remember even if life started on the wrong foot we serve an awesome God who is able to change any situation into a story and testimony which can be used to give others inspiration."

Summary:

I am sure most of us have either started at the bottom or things have happened to us in our life that we are not proud of which has set us back.

In this passage, God is saying no matter the negativity of the battles you have faced, even if unclean spirits have tried and attached themselves to you, He wants you to know that He is able to take all your life encounters and bring forth victory that not only will bring forth joy in your life, but also, will become quite an inspiration to help others with similar situations overcome their battles. So, I encourage you to submit to Him to get started today.

Reference Power Prayer

Dear Heavenly Father,

I release everything that has ever happened to me in Your hands. Every unpleasant encounter I have faced, all negativity I have overcame, even those times I have fought a painful battle are now released to You. I declare You are transforming everything for my good. Through Your power, I am a winner and every situation up until now has been a set up for me to receive a reward only You can place in my life. I declare my life is victorious and has become an inspiration to help others also overcome and win through Your mercy, grace, and favor in Jesus name, amen.

Chapter 13

Trusting in God Our Strength

Scripture reference:

He gives strength to the weary and increases the power of the weak.
Isaiah 40:29

Uplifting Quote:

"Sometimes strength is all you have not to be torn apart. Instead of allowing circumstances to shatter you, turn your direction to God who can mend, restore, protect, and perfect you exactly where you are in life."

Summary:

Instead of being frustrated; feeling torn apart, lean upon your Higher power and get strengthened by God who can bring forth order and refreshment your way.

Reference Power Prayer

Dear Heavenly Father,

Please cover me in Your strength. I feel weakened and need You to build me up. Give me restoration that only can be reached through You. I ask that You take every area I feel shattered and make it Whole as only You can in Jesus name, amen.

Scripture reference:

I can do all this through Him who gives me strength.
Philippians 4:13

Uplifting Quote:

"While going through different levels of natural and spiritual growth spurts, you may find that things hurt for a while but always remember that pain is part of growth and gaining strength."

Summary:

Stop looking at your pain, reacting and believing this is it by how you feel when God is always working in your life; mending you together stronger and greater than you were before. The pain is needed to grow strong as the qualified vessel He requires you to be so remain encouraged because things will get better.

Reference Power Prayer

Dear Heavenly Father,

As I go through different growth spurts and become whom You've called me to be, I ask You to be my strength in my weaknesses and allow Your mighty arm to hold me up; continue to keep me strong as I work on being the vessel You need. Thank you for keeping Your loving eye on me and never letting me go in Jesus name, amen.

Scripture references:

When hard pressed, I cried to the Lord; He brought me into a spacious place: The Lord is with me; I will not be afraid. What can mere mortals do to me?
Psalm 118:5, 6

"Be careful, or your hearts will be weighed down with carousing, drunkenness and the anxieties of life, and that day will close on you suddenly like a trap.
Luke 21:34

Trouble and distress have come upon me, but Your commands give me delight.
Psalm 119:143

Uplifting Quote:

"When facing a storm never stress yourself out because stress sometimes causes further issues including health problems which can potentially even lead to an early death so why not give God your stress and receive His rest today?"

Summary:

We were not created to carry stress, but sometimes we do it anyway and it acts as a chain which can harm our internal organs, causing us health problems and other problems which ultimately can even lead to death. God wants you to know that there is no reason to carry stress. Release it to Him and be on your way to receiving healing and restoration only granted through His love.

Reference Power Prayer

Dear Heavenly Father,

Please remove stress and worry out my life. Replace it with Your peace. Please heal my body of any damage that's attached due to stress. I desire to live the complete life You ordained me to live, and any harm my body suffered due to me trying to handle things on my own I ask that You forgive me and mend, restore, and make me Whole in Jesus name, amen.

Scripture references:

The LORD is my strength and my shield; my heart trusts in Him, and He helps me. My heart leaps for joy, and with my song I praise Him.
Psalm 28:7

You will keep in perfect peace all who trust in You, all whose thoughts are fixed on You!
Isaiah 26:3

Uplifting Quote:

"You may come across times where situations cause you to feel overwhelmed and it can alter your thought pattern. Just know that God loves you. Turn to His love, receive His power, trust in His timing. He can provide you with grace to overcome every battle you face. The presence of His healing power can show up in your circumstances as you trust in Him alone."

Summary:

Sometimes things happen in our lives which causes our mind to be driven into a multitude of directions. God led me to tell you today to release those unsettling thoughts in His hands, so that He can begin moving in your life.

Reference Power Prayer

Dear Heavenly Father,

Please remove any double mindedness I have. I ask You to clear my mind so that everything I must do shall flow freely. I thank you for releasing my best thoughts possible and granting me the victory, peace, and power that I need to overcome and win in Jesus name, amen.

Scripture reference:

The Sovereign Lord is my strength; He makes my feet like the feet of a deer, He enables me to tread on the heights.
Habakkuk 3:19

Uplifting Quote:

"There may be moments when you find yourself on this journey alone but be encouraged because that's the perfect time to submit to and spend time with God as you prepare to receive the blessings that He intended to bring forth in your life all along."

Summary:

I have recently faced this situation myself. Many times, when God is working on us, He requires a separation period where we must remove all distractions and fully dedicate ourselves to Him; total mind, body, and soul. My advice to you is when you find yourself in that season, get acquainted with God who will not only give you strength but will also send people in your life to help support you as you work to accomplish His will.

Reference Power Prayer

Dear Heavenly Father,

As I strive to reach where You intended me to be all along, and during my time of consecration, I ask You to help me keep my mind and heart attentive to Your will, focused on where You desire me to be; getting further acquainted with You so that I can begin accomplishing Your purpose. I thank you for sending me the support I need and always keeping me strengthened in Your love, in Jesus name, amen.

Scripture references:

The LORD is my strength and my shield; my heart trusts in Him, and He helps me. My heart leaps for joy, and with my song I praise Him.
Psalm 28:7

But you, Lord, do not be far from me. You are my strength; come quickly to help me.
Psalm 22:19

Lord, be gracious to us; we long for You. Be our strength every morning our salvation in time of distress.
Isaiah 33:2

Uplifting Quote:

"When the joy of the Lord is your strength, a peace revolves in your atmosphere and life in ways you can't imagine as you seek Him and believe."

Summary:

God covers you in His peace as you take refuge in His love and allow Him to be your comfort source.

Reference Power Prayer

Dear Heavenly Father,

Be my strength in the morning, afternoon, and evening. Keep me guarded in Your love. I know that only through Your love, peace, and protection everything shall be okay, so I am claiming it all right now in Jesus name, amen.

Scripture references:

"I have told you these things, so that in Me you may have peace. In this world you will have trouble. But take heart! I have overcome the world."
John 16:33

For this reason, I kneel before the Father.
Ephesians 3:14

Uplifting Quote:

"Never get discouraged by the trials that you face rather, turn to and trust in the Lord with all your heart to grant you peace and victory in your life, walk, and race as you trust in Him and believe."

Summary:

Kneeling before our Heavenly Father is key to breaking through every trial and being on the road to receiving complete victory. So, fight and win your battles on your knees today.

Reference Power Prayer

Dear Heavenly Father,

I kneel before You today and ask You to keep me comforted by Your love. Bring forth a wave of peace so that I don't get discouraged by what I must face, but rather, I will be in full alignment and receive the joy that only can be provided through You. Thank you for fighting and winning every battle for me as I kneel before Your Holy throne in Jesus mighty name, amen.

"No matter what storms may cross your path trust that God shall carry and protect you."
Angelica Lassiter

Chapter 14

Trusting in God Our Obstacle Fighter

Scripture reference:

When I said, "My foot is slipping," Your unfailing love, Lord, supported me.
Psalm 94:18

Uplifting Quote:

"There may be times when things appear unsteady and scary when you are facing the unknown, but, continue to trust the Lord with all your heart to bring forth victory in your life as He sits on His Holy throne."

Summary:

Even though you can't see the whole stairway, please trust in God to support your every step, uphold you in His hand, and lead you to that life of joy and peace He has planned as you believe.

Reference Power Prayer

Dear Heavenly Father,

I thank you for showing me through Your word and love that no matter how much it appears I may be slipping, Your support always has me covered. I love You and thank you for keeping me on steady and sturdy ground in Jesus name, amen.

Scripture reference:

My heart says of You, "Seek His face!" "Your face, Lord, I will seek"
Psalm 27:8

Uplifting Quote:

"There may be a lot of things going on in your life that you may not understand but one thing to always remember will never happen is God's unchanging hand and unfailing love leaving or forsaking you; stand confident in His love and trust that better days are coming."

Summary:

No matter what you're going through, always remember that God is keeping you safely planted in His hands. Press forth in His peace today. Seeking Him is always the best way to go because brightness is what follows those who love Him.

Reference Power Prayer

Dear Heavenly Father,

I may not understand what I am going through right now, but I will trust that You are right there beside me; You are guiding my every step. No matter how things appear, I trust that You are leading me to victory in Jesus name, amen.

Scripture reference:

Let us not become weary in doing good, for at the proper time we will reap a harvest if we do not give up.
Galatians 6:9

Uplifting Quote:

"One day things will fall in place according to God's will. Patience and gratitude while waiting is the key to receiving God's best intended blessings for your life."

Summary:

God is faithful and is faithfully shifting you towards a new level. Remain patient; continue to live righteously and trust Him to keep His word and fulfill His promises for your life.

Reference Power Prayer

Dear Heavenly Father,

I want to say thank you that everything I am facing right now is just a transition period to receive the things that are falling in place for me. I thank you for giving me victory. I will be patient while You are setting me up to live the best life I possibly can in Jesus mighty name, amen.

Scripture references:

But the Lord is faithful, and He will strengthen you and protect you from the evil one.
2 Thessalonians 3:3

No weapon formed against you shall prosper, and every tongue which rises against you in judgment You shall condemn. 'This is the heritage of the servants of the Lord, and their righteousness is from Me," Says the Lord.
Isaiah 54:17

Uplifting Quotes:

"Protection from God is surely protection that will last."

No matter what you are facing, always remember that God is our battle warrior, so I encourage you to declare:

"I know that God would never give me more than I am able to handle so I choose to be happy regardless."

Summary:

There's no greater protection than what is poured through God, so I encourage you to accept His invitation to place His hands upon your life.

Reference Power Prayer

Dear Heavenly Father,

I just want to say thank you for protecting me and keeping me fully equipped and covered by the shielding blood of Jesus hallelujah, amen!!

Scripture reference:

In all this you greatly rejoice, though now for a little while you may have had to suffer grief in all kinds of trials: These have come so that the proven genuineness of your faith—of greater worth than gold, which perishes even though refined by fire—may result in praise, glory and honor when Jesus Christ is revealed.
1 Peter 1:6, 7

Uplifting Quote:

"If you are going through a tough season in your life, I encourage you to seek God because two things will happen: either the storm will supernaturally diminish, or He will give you supernatural strength until He is finished with the required purpose of the storm. Always remember that God's love surpasses all things."

Summary:

We will all face times when we wonder if God is going to give us favor but I want to encourage you to think of the storms like a cycle in a washing machine and believe that God is cleansing you and supernaturally moving you forward into a greater purpose than before. Trust Him; He has so much in store for your life.

Reference Power Prayer

Dear Heavenly Father,

As I am facing this tough season, I ask You to grant me the wisdom, discernment, and revelation I need so that not only will I come out of this situation like pure gold, but I shall accomplish the intended purpose for this storm. I thank you for what You have already done and are about to do in my life in Jesus name, amen.

Scripture reference:

Your unfailing love, O LORD, is as vast as the heavens;
Your faithfulness reaches beyond the clouds:
Your righteousness is like the mighty mountains, Your
justice like the ocean depths. You care for people and
animals alike, O LORD:
How precious is Your unfailing love, O God! All
humanity finds shelter in the shadow of Your wings.
Psalm 36:5, 6, 7

Uplifting Quote:

*"Always remember that there is no failure in God; as long as
we keep Him in our center, the storms may come but they will
never cause destruction to us, maybe a little shake but not a
particle falling off."*

Summary:

God is the greatest power source. His grace and power
is sufficient and able to prevent us from failing as we
cling on to His mighty hand every day of our lives.
Trust Him!

Reference Power Prayer

Dear Heavenly Father,

While facing raging storms, please keep me blanketed,
protected, and covered by You. Allow me to keep hold
of Jesus's garment as I wait for the storms to pass
through my life in Jesus powerful name, amen.

Chapter 15

Inspiration About Your Value

Introduction:

Below are quotes I've written about your value and how valuable God sees you.

Scripture reference:

I praise You because I am fearfully and wonderfully made; Your works are wonderful, I know that full well. **Psalm 139:14**

Uplifting Quote:

If you don't find value in yourself then nobody else will.

Summary:

The moment when we realize our true worth and the masterpiece we were created to be is when we will begin to see people presented in our life who we can value and who will also value us the way we deserve to be valued.

Reference Power Prayer

Dear Heavenly Father,

Please show me how to love myself the way You created me to be loved. I declare I am a unique individual with a unique purpose and my purpose and all things that I set my mind to do shall be fulfilled in Jesus name, amen.

Scripture reference:

I will give thanks to You, LORD, with all my heart; I will tell of all Your wonderful deeds.
Psalm 9:1

Uplifting Quote:

One thing we are unable to do is replace what only God can give us so regardless of what you may be lacking or missing in your life, I encourage you to wake up every morning and say-

"Thank you Lord for a new day and for giving me things I am unable to get on my own which are only supplied through You. If there is anything else I am lacking or missing in my life then I ask that I receive it immediately in Jesus name, amen!"

Summary:

This is a great declaration God gave me to help you work towards not only receiving a supply of all your needs but also, being able to help with being whom He created you to be.

Reference Power Prayer

Dear Heavenly Father,

I am not going to ask You for anything, rather, I am going to take some time to say- *"Thank You Lord for being my everything!!"*. You indeed deserve all the glory, honor, and praise forever in Jesus name, amen.

Scripture references:

See, I have engraved you on the palms of My hands; your walls are ever before Me.
Isaiah 49:16

For we are God's handiwork, created in Christ Jesus to do good works, which God prepared in advance for us to do.
Ephesians 2:10

Uplifting Quote:

"Despite how invaluable you are to others, God is waiting to show you just how priceless and wonderfully made you are, as you seek Him with your whole heart and believe, so seek Him today."

Summary:

What God sees in you is so much more than what is recognizable. It is far beyond the human eye view; He is waiting to show you your true worth, so I encourage you to allow Him to by letting Him lead you to be your best version possible.

Reference Power Prayer

Dear Heavenly Father,

I thank you for the unique value You have given me. Please help me identify and discover my hidden talents so that I can be the best version of myself possible in Jesus name, amen.

Chapter 16

Trusting in Our God Who Gives Us Healing

Scripture reference

He heals the brokenhearted and binds up their wounds.
Psalm 147:3

Uplifting Quote:

"When pain attempts to ruin your day, allow your hope, faith, and confidence in God to alleviate your sorrows in every form and way as you believe."

Summary:

Pain can become joy when God is the reason for your joy. He is endlessly able to give you countless joy once you submit to His purpose and will. Submit to His will for your life so that He can mend your pain.

Reference Power Prayer

Dear Heavenly Father,

I ask that You completely heal brokenness and pain out my life. Bind me up with Your comfort, restore me with Your peace, and direct me to Your purpose. Please remove every mask that is trying to cover me up in failure in Jesus name, amen.

Chapter 17

Overcoming Painful Situations Through Our God of Healing

Scripture reference:

He heals the brokenhearted and binds up their wounds.
Psalm 147:3

Uplifting Quotes:

"Broken moments can become restored moments when you allow God to do the mending together of them."

"Wounded moments can become healed moments when you allow God to be the source of healing. Seek God for healing."

Summary:

God is waiting to heal every broken area of your life and show you through His love, joy, and favor everything will be alright, so confidently receive His healing today. There is no point walking around feeling half fulfilled when God is waiting to mend, restore, protect, heal, and see you through it all.

Reference Power Prayer

Dear Heavenly Father,

I ask You to heal every broken area in my life. Give me total restoration, joy, peace, and blessings as only You can in Jesus name, amen.

Scripture references:

For I am the LORD your God who takes hold of your right hand and says to you, "Do not fear; I will help you."
Isaiah 41:13

Cast all your anxiety on Him because He cares for you.
1 Peter 5:7

Uplifting Quotes:

"The most painful situations can bring forth the most joy-filled creations when you allow God to do the healing."

"When things seem to be falling apart they are actually falling into place if you allow God to do the mending together of the foundation."

Summary:

Let God heal your pain; let it go so that restoration can show up and flow.

Reference Power Prayer

Dear Heavenly Father,

As I seek You through this prayer, I ask that You step in and heal my pain, heal my anxiety, and allow everything to fall in place for me through Your everlasting love, joy, peace, and mending power in Jesus name, amen.

Chapter 18

Giving Thanks to God, Our Peace

Scripture reference:

Peace I leave with you; My peace I give you. I do not give to you as the world gives. Do not let your hearts be troubled and do not be afraid.
John 14:27

Uplifting Quote:

"If you entrust God with your now (the present), then He can bring peace in your life as only He can as you seek Him to receive it."

Summary:

I encourage you to take this scripture as a reminder that His peace is poured upon your life and will keep you covered regardless.

Reference Power Prayer

Dear Heavenly Father,

Thank you for the peace that is poured through Your love. I ask You to continue keeping me surrounded in Your peace regardless of what I face. I am confident that You will keep Your promise to always be there for me, so I thank you for lavishing me with Your peace forever in Jesus name, amen.

Chapter 19

Submitting and Surrendering All

Scripture references:

But seek first His kingdom and His righteousness, and all these things will be given to you as well.
Matthew 6:33

Commit to the Lord whatever you do, and He will establish your plans.
Proverbs 16:3

He must become greater; I must become less."
John 3:30

Uplifting Quotes:

"Always remember besides your immediate family to place God first in your life."

"Build a relationship with God and allow your stress to transform to His rest."

Summary:

God is first and He's irreplaceable so please make sure that you're keeping Him as a priority in your life because He loves you and honors your acknowledgement of His presence. I speak from personal experience that He is right there by your side, He is your best friend and if you take time daily to allow Him in your life, you will discover a new journey with Him that can't be obtained anywhere else shall begin.

Reference Power Prayer

Dear Heavenly Father,

I ask for Your help with balance in my life so that You can be the center of my life. I would like to seek You first and have everything else fall into place according to Heaven's standards in Jesus name, amen.

Scripture references:

"Before I formed you in the womb I knew you, before you were born I set you apart; I appointed you as a Prophet to the nations."
Jeremiah 1:5

For I know the thoughts that I think toward you, says the Lord, thoughts of peace and not of evil, to give you a future and a hope.
Jeremiah 29:11

Uplifting Quote:

"There is so much that God has ordained and planted inside of you so why not turn in His direction in prayer and invite His will into your life, so that not only will you see your own personal goals and desires come forth but also, you will discover what is only available through His might, plans for you, and amazing power shall manifest."

Summary:

God already had plans for you before you were formed in your mother's womb so why not take this opportunity for every unknown possibility to show up in your life and bloom. Ask God to help you discover your purpose today.

Reference Power Prayer

Dear Heavenly Father,

I ask You to help me discover my ordained purpose which was established before I was formed in my mother's womb. Lead me in the way to go so that every opportunity You have lined up for me to complete can be accomplished. I love You and can't wait to receive those things you have appointed for me to fulfill in Jesus name, amen.

Scripture references:

We are hard pressed on every side, but not crushed; perplexed, but not in despair: Persecuted, but not abandoned; struck down, but not destroyed.
2 Corinthians 4:8, 9

Why are you in despair, my soul? Why are you disturbed within me? Hope in God, because I will praise Him once again, since His presence saves me and He is my God.
Psalm 43:5

For you are my hope, Lord God, my security since I was young.
I depended on you since birth, when you brought me from my mother's womb; I praise you continuously.
Psalm 71:5-6

Uplifting Quote:

"God has a great plan for your life. Never define your valley, still moments, or preparation season with settling in believing that He is not going to open up doors for you. Just because it may be stormy right now does not mean sunshine isn't around the corner."

Summary:

God is forever moving and making things new. We are constantly reminded of this even through the seasons and seeing nature change so please take this as a reminder that just because you are in your growing season doesn't mean that you are never going to reach your full-fledged potential.

Reference Power Prayer

Dear Heavenly Father,

As I face this moment in the desert, I want to let You know that I trust in You. I believe in You. I believe that You are transforming my situation for my good so thank you in advance for pouring rain upon all my dry places in Jesus name, amen.

Scripture reference:

Turn my eyes from worthless things and give me life through Your word.
Psalm 119:37

Uplifting Quote:

"The only way to truly have peace, joy, hope, and happiness in your life is to turn away from the confusion and disarray of the world and become embraced by the only one who has numbered all your days. Seek God today. He still performs miracles and is all that you need."

Summary:

There is nothing that this world can offer you that God is not able to give you in greater form so stop looking for quick fixes and get all your needs fulfilled through the supplier of every source.

Reference Power Prayer

Dear Heavenly Father,

I ask You to help me take my mind and focus off things which are worthless to me and my purpose. Help me to obey Your word and become that bright vessel You created me to be in Jesus name, amen.

Scripture reference:

For no matter how many promises God has made, they are "Yes" in Christ. And so through Him the "Amen" is spoken by us to the glory of God.
2 Corinthians 1:20

Uplifting Quote:

"The blessings of God are Yes and Amen so why not submit to His will and ways so that your every heart desire shall begin to unfold as you seek Him?"

Summary:

He has so much planned, so seek Him and be on your way to receiving the great things that He has in store for you.

Reference Power Prayer

Dear Heavenly Father,

I ask that every promise that has been spoken out of Your mouth as mine starts to unfold and manifest RIGHT NOW in Jesus name, amen!

Chapter 20

Resisting the Devil

Scripture references:

No temptation has overtaken you except what is common to mankind. And God is faithful; He will not let you be tempted beyond what you can bear. But when you are tempted, He will also provide a way out so that you can endure it.
1 Corinthians 10:13

Be sober, be vigilant; because your adversary the devil walks about like a roaring lion, seeking whom he may devour.
1 Peter 5:8

There is a way that appears to be right, but in the end it leads to death.
Proverbs 14:12

The thief comes only to steal and kill and destroy. I came that they may have life and have it abundantly.
John 10:10

Uplifting Quote:

"If you are waiting on God never get impatient and go your own way because, you may be led into a trap which will hinder your path and purpose by Satan."

Summary:

There is a way which seems right to us but it's actually the devil trying to lead us to destruction. I encourage you not to allow him to. Seek God for discernment and rebuke the devil's attacks in advance.

Reference Power Prayer

Dear Heavenly Father,

Please give me the patience I need to wait on You, discernment to recognize any opportunity that was not sent by you, and determination not to fall for any of the devil's wicked schemes in Jesus name, amen.

Scripture reference:

"Behold, I have given you authority to tread on serpents and scorpions, and over all the power of the enemy, and nothing will injure you.
Luke 10:19

Uplifting Quote:

"Anyone who is presently in a spiritual battle and the devil is trying to push you over the edge always remember, that the devil can only harass us but if you are walking with God, He will only permit Satan to do so much. You have to have a mindset that decides no matter what you will walk with and trust in God until the end and believe He will never fail you and that the best is yet to come."

Summary:

You got to take authority and let the enemy know that God's in charge and will help you win and overcome all that you encounter in your life.

Reference Power Prayer

Dear Heavenly Father,

While facing the enemy's attacks, I ask You to help me not be ignorant to his devices. Rather, I ask that You help me to just brush him aside and walk as the victorious vessel You have created me to be in Jesus name, amen.

Scripture reference:

Submit therefore to God. Resist the devil and he will flee from you.
James 4:7

Uplifting Quotes:

"The devil will try and torment your mind and make you feel unneeded, overlooked, and unimportant. I encourage you to ignore him and continue shining like the gem God created you to be and keep seeking Him with your whole heart.

"Always remember that the enemy only comes to kill, steal, and destroy, but God is right there at all times and waiting to grant you multitudes of peace, deliverance, protection and joy as you stand strong and submit to His will."

Summary:

I encourage you to act like you don't even know the enemy. Wake up every day and speak positivity and that you already know you are winning with Christ on your side. Then He will flee.

Reference Power Prayer

Dear Heavenly Father,

I declare as the devil attempts to tell me who I am, I will remind myself of who he is and where his end will be. I will do Your work in total confidence as I trample the enemy underneath my feet in Jesus name, amen.

Scripture reference:

Submit therefore to God. Resist the devil and he will flee from you.

James 4:7

Uplifting Quote:

"Just when the devil thinks that He has you depressed and down, God is able to step in and change things all around in your favor so claim victory over every single attack of the enemy today."

Summary:

God's favor overpowers all that you face. Let God know that you trust in Him today by sealing your belief with a praise.

Reference Power Prayer

Dear Heavenly Father,

I declare I am walking into the promises You have for me; my joy has been reconciled and rejuvenated as I am trusting in Your love and resisting the enemy's attacks and lies in Jesus name, amen.

Chapter 21

Prophetic Declarations

Introduction:

These declarations were given through the Holy Spirit for you to speak in your atmosphere for a greater walk with God.

1)   *"I declare everything pertaining to my life IS BLESSED from the moment that I was born until I one day rest, every single thing pertaining to my life and generations to come IS BLESSED in Jesus powerful name, amen!!"*

2)   *"I was created to achieve great things, so I declare it shall be so in Jesus name, I shall soar!!!!"*

Summary:

You must believe it in order to receive it so speak with power, stay empowered, and I believe it shall be awesomely seen in your life.

Chapter 22

Believe the Best Is Yet to Come

Introduction:

This chapter has quotes along with summaries I've written to help you be inspired that where you've been is nothing compared to where God is bringing you to.

1)   *"No matter how hard your day or even your life has been always remember, God is not finished with you yet. Your best days are still ahead of you. Trust in God wholeheartedly that He has an awesome plan for your life."*

Summary:

Just because you're facing a difficult season please remember, God is daily revising your life to His version of joy, peace and favor, just trust in Him enough to receive it.

2)   *"Taking the first step in moving forward may be hard but know that God has your life displayed in His book and safely planted in the palm of His hands. He is there at all times, directing and positioning you to reach heights which can amaze you if you believe. Be led by the will and desire of God and be led to success."*

Summary:

Even an airplane takes a little pressure to take flight so encourage yourself that according to God's plans that things are about to change a greater level.

3)   *"No matter how difficult things may get I encourage you to keep pressing forward. Your best days are still ahead of you. Stand strong and confident in Jesus; He will push you up and pull you out of your droughts so stay encouraged."*

Summary:

Please take a few moments and embrace with confidence the new and great things that are about to happen in your life through your faith activating God's power!!

Chapter 23

New Beginnings through Christ

Scripture reference:

Though your beginning was small, yet your latter end would increase abundantly.
Job 8:7

Uplifting Quote:

"God is able to give you a head start even when you haven't begun your journey yet."

Summary:

Many times, you're in the process of trying to discover your journey when God already has your journey lined up, but you must do your part and invite Him in your life.

Uplifting Quote:

"You may not have had a great start in life, but God is waiting to give you a great finish as you seek Him with your whole heart and believe."

Summary:

God wants you to know that yes, you may have started off underachieved, under-accomplished, and small, but if you would just seek His plan, He is not only able to direct you to a greater purpose, but He is also able to allow you to recover all as you submit to Him. So I encourage you to diligently seek and trust in Him today.

Uplifting Quote:

"Always try your best to be who God asked you to be and trust that He shall lead you to victory."

Summary:

Time and time again we are advised to obey the will of God but sometimes we get nervous because it seems He's not going to either allow us to fulfill what He asked us to do or while we were trying to fulfill the task it failed. God is saying today to turn back His way and trust Him to lead your path.

Reference Power Prayer

Dear Heavenly Father,

Up until this point, I've found myself not fully able to achieve the life Your word promises me. I would like to have access to the joy and life only available through You so today, I ask You to order my steps and transform me into the creation You have ordained me to be as I strive to reach my destiny in Jesus name, amen.

Time on this Earth is Limited

Scripture reference:

A man's days are numbered. You know the number of His months. He cannot live longer than the time You have set.

Job 14:5

Uplifting Quote:

"We all have an expiration date on Earth and since none of us know when that time will come I encourage you to consider giving your life to Christ so that you know your next life is secure in the hands of God."

<u>Invitation to Give Your Life to Christ</u>

If this book has blessed and encouraged you, I invite you to allow God to be a daily part of your life through a relationship with Him; He can begin removing your sorrows and filling you up with joy, peace and every ounce of assurance and love that you will ever need.

If you have never given your life to Jesus or desire rededication to Him, I am offering a chance to do it today. I have enclosed a simple prayer below for you to speak to confess your sins and give your life to Christ.

Sinner's Prayer

Dear Heavenly Father,

"This is me and You know me better than anyone else knows me. You know my sorrows, You know my pain, and every error I have made both knowingly and unknowingly, even those things I cannot name. Father, I ask You today to forgive me for my sins. You say in Your written word that if I believe in my heart and confess with my mouth that Jesus Christ died on the cross and was raised from the dead on the third day that I shall be saved. Lord, today I confess my sins and ask You to lead me to the path of righteousness today and forever. Thank you for saving me naturally and eternally in Jesus name, amen!"

"If you declare with your mouth, "Jesus is Lord," and believe in your heart that God raised Him from the dead, you will be saved."
Romans 10:9

If you said this prayer with faith and belief in your heart, you have just been saved. I encourage you to connect with other believers, find a BIBLE based church home and further your growth and relationship with God and His love will take you places that you have never been before.

He has done this for me and can do it for you, there is absolutely nothing that His amazing love can't make possible for you if you just believe. God bless and take care everybody!!!

For God so loved the world that He gave His one and only Son, that whoever believes in Him shall not perish but have eternal life.
John 3:16

ABOUT THE AUTHOR

Angelica Lassiter was born in Providence, Rhode Island, USA. She was brought up in church most of her life.

While serving God, she discovered a gift of writing where spiritual poetry and encouragements became part of her life. God uses her to write inspiration every day.

She shares her quotes in this book and looks forward to helping others also discover their inner strength, abilities, the true power of God, and the love that He has for them. She enjoys spending her quality time with her children and helping others.

Angelica's book, Confidence in God is a book of encouragement and inspiration that describes our Confidence to overcome challenges that head our way through trusting in God alone. Available at all major merchants.

Angelica can be reached on her website www.gracedinspirations.com where she shares her testimony and you can find more inspiration, provide feedback, see upcoming events, purchase products, and contact her directly.

Made in the USA
Columbia, SC
27 March 2021